AND THEY SHALL BE ONE FLESH

This book is prescriptive in nature, using the Bible as its reference point. It seeks to examine the phrase "And they shall be one flesh" with the objective of correcting anomalies in the marriage institution that are not in line with the Bible. It is believed that this book would bless every marriage, to the betterment of all.

*I dedicate this book to the glory of God and to my husband.
I thank God for what He has done to transform our
marriage to the standard of His calling.*

AND THEY SHALL BE ONE FLESH

T. O. Oluwadare

ARTHUR H. STOCKWELL LTD.
Elms Court   Ilfracombe   Devon
Established 1898

© T. O. Oluwadare, 1997
First published in Great Britain, 1997

All rights reserved.
No part of this publication may be reproduced
or transmitted in any form or by any means,
electronic or mechanical, including photocopy,
recording, or any information storage and
retrieval system, without permission
in writing from the copyright holder.

British Library Cataloguing-in-Publication Data.
A catalogue record for this book is available
from the British Library.

ISBN 0 7223 3057-X

Printed in Great Britain by
Arthur H. Stockwell Ltd.
Elms Court   Ilfracombe
Devon

CONTENTS

INTRODUCTION 7

Chapter One
PREREQUISITE TO BECOMING ONE FLESH 9

Chapter Two
"CAN TWO WALK TOGETHER,
EXCEPT THEY BE AGREED?"
Amos 3:3 14

Chapter Three
FORCES WORKING AGAINST ONE FLESH 21

Chapter Four
ONE FLESH 32

CONCLUSION 36

INTRODUCTION

The Bible in Genesis, Chapter 2:24 says **"Therefore shall a man leave his father and his mother, and shall cleave unto his wife: and they shall be one flesh."**

What does it mean to *cleave*? According to Webster's dictionary, cleave means — 'To be part of, to adhere, to hold fast to, to stick to'. After such a meaningful and far-reaching word like cleave, the Bible went on further to say *'and they shall be one flesh'*. This shows that to cleave alone is not descriptive of the heart of the Almighty concerning marriage. After staying together, adhering together, and holding fast to each other, God still insists that a couple should be one flesh.

By inference therefore, we can conclude that *'and they shall be one flesh'* is a resultant factor, and a consequence of the cleaving. Therefore the cleaving together of a man and his wife, is a prerequisite to becoming one flesh.

The steps can be explained as follows:

Step I: A man shall leave his father and mother.
Step II: He shall cleave unto his wife, (stick, hold fast, adhere).
Step III: And they shall be one flesh.

For the purpose of this book, we shall examine the phrase *'and they shall be one flesh'* which is a commandment of God.

Chapter One

PREREQUISITE TO BECOMING ONE FLESH

However, before any man can implement a commandment of God, there needs to be put in place two things. In the first place, you need to be born again; this means accepting Jesus Christ into your life as your Lord and Saviour. John 14:6. ***"Jesus saith unto him, I am the way, the truth, and the life: no man cometh unto the Father, but by me."*** Also without being born again, you can never be able to implement any commandment of God. John 3:3 says ***"Jesus answered and said unto him, Verily, verily, I say unto thee, Except a man be born again, he cannot see the kingdom of God."*** This means **you can not enjoy the peace of the kingdom which comes by obeying God's commandment, if you are not born again.** 1 John 3:9 says ***"Whosoever is born of God doth not commit sin; for his seed remaineth in him: and he cannot sin, because he is born of God."*** It is impossible for you to obey God's commandment if you are not born of God.

Secondly, after being born again, you need to renew your mind and body by the word of God; that is you lay down your will and say "Lord, not my will, but thine be done." Romans 12:1-2 says ***"I*** *beseech you therefore, brethren, by the mercies of God, that ye present your bodies a living sacrifice, holy, acceptable unto God, which is your reasonable service."* It goes on to say *". . . be not conformed to this world: but be ye transformed by the renewing of your mind, that ye may prove what is that good, and acceptable, and perfect, will of God."* Your body must become a living sacrifice. The word of God must transform you before you can do the perfect will of God. It is possible to be born again but not renewed in your mind. You are what is called a carnal Christian and the Bible says in Romans 8:7 *"Because the carnal mind is enmity against God: for it is not subject to the law of God, neither indeed can be."* You can be born again, but if you are carnal, if your mind is not renewed by God's words, you can never be subject to the law/commandments of God. You can try but it would be impossible for you to attain, because you are still in the flesh.

It is important to put these two steps in place, by any couple who plan to obey God in the area of becoming one flesh, like all other commandments if they do not handle the two prerequisites they have planned to fail. They must be born again, and they must be renewed by the word of God, before they can hope to obey successfully any commandments of God. Because the only people who can be one flesh with each other, are those who are dead to flesh. You can be born again, but if you are not dead to flesh; you can attempt to cleave to your spouse, but not in the way dictated by God, and you can never be one flesh with your spouse. Ephesians 5:25-26 says *"Husbands, love your wives, even as Christ also loved the church, and gave himself*

for it" . . . ***"That he might sanctify and cleanse it with the washing of water by the word."*** Using the example of our Lord Jesus Christ in verse 25, a man must give himself for his wife; forget his flesh, bury flesh before he can be able to sanctify his wife and cleanse her with the washing by the word.

To be successful in the commandment of being one flesh, the mind, the will and the emotions of the couple must be completely renewed by the word of God, then they can obey him in this as well as other commandments.

There are many people whose minds are still conformed to the world or their emotions dictated by the world's standard: i.e., what they see in novels, romance, etc. Their wills are still strong and self-will has not given way to God's will. Such people can never be one flesh. Let us look at an example to show a carnal Christian, whose flesh and worldly standard control, and a spiritual Christian whose heart has been renewed and transformed by the word of God. The heart is made up of mind, will and emotion; let us see how these three things can be affected.

Two women have husbands who shout at them when giving out instructions in anger.

CARNAL CHRISTIAN:

(1) **Mind:** Shout back at him.

(2) **Will:** I am a wife not a servant, if he can't talk politely, I will do what I want, he cannot push me around.

(3) **Emotion:** He is not romantic, he is not cherishing me, if he doesn't love me, he will get the worst from me.

CHRISTIAN RENEWED BY THE WORD:

(1) **Mind:** It is written 'Follow peace with all men, also the fruit of righteousness is sown in peace'.

(2) **Will:** It is written, 'Submit unto thy husband, as unto the Lord, whatever he asks me to do I must do'. Once it is not contrary to my belief in God.

(3) **Emotion:** It is written 'Love suffers long, and I love him therefore whatever he does. God will perfect him. I will pray to God his maker to perfect the good works he has started'.

We can see that from the reaction of the sister renewed by the word of God, the fire would be quenched. As she obeys her husband and shows him in quietness, that work of the devil in him, will not be able to operate. The Bible says we should not be overcome with evil but we should overcome evil with good. This is a divine truth when light shines into darkness without doubt darkness must disappear. As children of light, if we walk in the light, we will always overcome the enemy. The devil will not be able to comprehend our actions. The Bible says ye are light, and our father is light, we are his children. Hence when we walk as light, we are walking in dominion. The devil can never comprehend us.

We can only defeat the devil by walking in the

spirit and by the word of God. If you use human wisdom, you will always be defeated. The devil is the father of earthly wisdom and he will overcome you if you use your carnal wisdom. James 3:17 says ***"But the wisdom that is from above is first pure, then peaceable, gentle, and easy to be entreated, full of mercy and good fruits, without partiality, and without hypocrisy."*** It is only through the wisdom from above, derived from the word of God, that you can be one flesh. This wisdom is recognised by its fruits; without this wisdom transforming your mind and its principles guiding you, you cannot be one flesh. This wisdom means application of the word of God. The word of God teaches us all the things above; i.e., being full of mercy and good fruits, etc. When you are renewed by the word of God (Bible — which is God's manual of operation) it would be possible to be successful in your Christian life and to walk according to God's instructions, part of which is to be one flesh with your spouse.

Chapter Two

"CAN TWO WALK TOGETHER, EXCEPT THEY BE AGREED?" Amos 3:3

To become one flesh, God is asking a couple to do more than walk together. As it is written, that two cannot even walk together, except they agree. Hence what a couple needs, is a super agreement; to make two become one. How can two become one? By communication, by adaptation and by conformity. It takes a dedication, a devotion to a course and a complete reorientation to make two become one.

If a couple are doing more than walk together, i.e., by living together, sharing everything, having the same vision, the same ideas, etc., we can see that the most important aspect of marriage is in agreement. Agreement is the power force of the marriage. You can determine whatever you want together and pray it into existence by agreement. Matthew 18:19 says ***"Again I say unto you, That if two of you shall agree on earth as touching any thing that they shall ask, it shall be done for them of my Father which is in heaven."*** Therefore, the gift of agreement is a great gift God has given every married couple. This gift can ultimately ensure the success of the marriage or the downfall of the marriage if neglected or misused.

The first two years of marriage, which are the first years of adjustment, are supposed to be geared towards finding a point of agreement. That is every area of your life must be made open. You must be naked before each other and not ashamed. Genesis 2:25 says *"And they were both naked, the man and his wife, and were not ashamed."*

When applying open communication, a point of agreement must be found for every issue. This in itself is part of the process of cleaving. Two lives must be interwoven into each other, past, present and future, and a joint focus must be taken concerning most issues.

A family is the smaller unit of a nation. A nation according to Webster's dictionary is 'a body of people recognised as an entity'. It is a people united under a particular political organisation, usually occupying a defined territory. Looking at the above meaning, we can see that a family is a type of small nation, and every nation has Government policies and National objectives. Thus in every family, there must be several meetings like there is done in Government, where all the pressure groups bring their opinion; and after all are looked at, there are corporate objectives taking care of every individual interest.

The same way a family must have objectives and policies. When there are children, these objectives should be enlarged to take care of their own interest. To fail to plan, is to plan to fail. Most marriages fail because couples refuse to do their responsibilities by planning their future. To play with your life and your future, is to refuse to have policies and objectives.

Policies: Are selected and planned lines of conduct by which individual decisions are made and co-ordination is achieved.

Objectives: Are aims or goals of a group having an existence external to the observer.

A nation that refuses to listen to the pressure groups and take care of their interests, is already sitting on a keg of dynamite that can explode, because it is practising repression. The same way the head of a family that refuses to take care of the interests of his wife and children, is repressing them and cannot enjoy the full potential that God has deposited in them. From a relatively young age, children should be encouraged to express their yearnings and complaints, and the parents hold it a duty to explain the reasons for certain decisions to justify themselves, or to adapt the aspirations of the child to the objectives of the family.

In all the above, God's will should guide the decisions of the family; and the final decision lies with the husband, who should be under the direction of our Lord Jesus Christ. God's will must guide him, not the wife's will, or the children's tantrums. This is why the father, as the head of the family, needs to be grounded in the word of God, so that he can apply the knowledge to guide his family aright. If the mother is grounded too, it makes the job more easier, because her advice should be quality advice confirmed and supported by the word of God.

The following are some of the issues that must be agreed on by the couple. Please note that these are just examples, every area must be trashed out, no area is too inconsequential. The area you neglect could be the area that the devil will use to penetrate in years to come. Therefore you must look into every aspect of your life. But for the purpose of this book, we will look at the following important areas, which must be adjusted to fit the new status of being married.

FRIENDS:
Every friend must be discussed in terms of history, of friendship contribution to the life of the spouse, who is the friend, etc. Both parties should discuss the approach to handle such friendship in future. If there is a personalised friendship that cannot be turned unto a family friend, such friendship must be reviewed. The Bible says what God has joined together let no man put asunder. If such friendship is allowed to foster, it will eventually put the marriage asunder, because it refuses to recognise the unity of flesh. Therefore all friendships must be adjusted to encompass the couple and the information must be clearly communicated to such friends, so that they can get conformed to the idea that there is a change of status and they must adapt to this change.

FAMILY:
The families must be discussed and adjusted. Approach to each side, wife/husband side must be decided. Usually same approach cannot be adopted, because the historical background usually differs. Some families are educated, others illiterate; some are closely knit, others are distant. Each family has

its own peculiarities, the same way each individual in the family has his/her own peculiarities and principles. Therefore it is impossible to have a blanket attitude to handle family relationships. Hence a couple must discuss these issues and decide on how to deal with the families and the individuals in them. By so doing, the wife already has a dosier on each member of her husband's family and does not need to go through the unnecessary hardship of learning by experience. The husband also, on his own part, would understand the wife's family expectations of him and how he can forge relationships easily with the members of the family. If two must become one flesh, what is in the husband must be transferred to the wife and vice versa, so that they can walk in agreement as well as establish a formidable force that cannot be penetrated by intrigues of the in-laws. They must be seen to have the same policy, friends in the families.

WORK:

Your work must be discussed; your boss, your colleagues, the salary, hours of work, demand, fears and even inadequacies must be discussed. Any work that demands so much time that leads to the neglect of your children, is not from God. It is a gift of the devil to destroy you. Many great men learnt the lessons very late in life and regretted it when it was too late. If you devote your youth, your best years to a job or in making money, and you neglect your wife and children, you would have managed to ruin all the lives associated with you. Jeremiah 1:16 says **"And I will utter my judgments against** *them touching all their wickedness, who have forsaken me, and have burnt incense unto other gods, and worshipped the works of their own hands."*

It is possible to worship the work of your hand, if your work prevents you from serving God the way you should, or performing your responsibilities to your family. You would also have managed to frustrate your spouse; he/she might become frustrated, cling to his/her children or somebody else; create a world for himself/herself; could be business, friendship or even church activities. You then have in your hands a man/woman you married from youth, with a zest for life, transformed into a lifeless individual, who has lost the zest of living and is merely existing; or on the other hand, if he/she was not born again, he/she could be lured into adultery, to find companionship; persons to discuss with and relate with. Furthermore, your children might grow up without a father/mother counselling influence. They could be children who would sell all that their parents had worked for.

Hence both the wife and husband must scrutinise their work, find out that it supplies their needs; but the hours should be that which would ensure that God's programme for your lives is achieved. God wants you to dominate your environment. Genesis 1:27-28 says *"So God created man in his own image, in the image of God created he him; male and female created he them . . . And God blessed them, and God said unto them, Be fruitful, and multiply, and replenish the earth, and subdue it; and have dominion over the fish of the sea, and over the fowl of the air, and over every living*

thing that moveth upon the earth. " You are to dominate all things, not one thing. It is immature for any man or woman to cling to a job at the expense of his home and future and God's plan for his life.

CHURCH OR SOCIAL ACTIVITIES:
Church activities must be discussed if the couple are not born again; social activities must be discussed. Some churches, through their activities, encourage separation of couples; this should not be done. We should not be unaware of the wiles of the devil. If God says a couple are one flesh, the church should recognise them as such. Furthermore, some couples use church activities to create another life for themselves, either because of neglect by spouse, or other reasons. They create friendship as a fall-back on, because of their unhappy family situation. This is why issues should be discussed not avoided. One must examine motive for services, and be sure one's works have record in heaven, and one is just not an escapist. Church activities should help the marriage not put pressure on it. Hence every mature couple must discuss it.

Other areas are hobbies, children, social activities. Two must agree and the process of two agreeing to become one is the process of cleaving together. It is only after there is agreement, that a family can walk together in one unity of mind and purpose. However, like the Bible says, the kingdom of God suffers violence. There are forces that try to oppose the will of God for couples, that they should be one flesh and one can only attain with a ruthless, determination to obey God, and to overcome all the contrary forces.

Chapter Three

FORCES WORKING AGAINST ONE FLESH

The divorce rate is going higher daily in nations; some are refusing to marry and many that are married are in enslavement; all these are not in accordance with the plan of God for man. Genesis 2:24 says *"Therefore shall a man leave his father and mother, and shall cleave unto his wife: and they shall be one flesh."*

There are tears and broken hearts in many marriages; many are disillusioned, the marriage institution is failing. Those that are Christians, live in marriage by enduring rather than enjoying their marriage. Why? There are two kinds of forces working against a couple becoming one flesh: (a) internal forces, (b) external forces.

INTERNAL FORCES:
There are internal forces affecting the unity of the home within the nuclear family, i.e. father and mother and children. These forces are differences in the make up of the individuals in the family. We will examine them below:

The difference in physiological make up of a man and a woman — God said that a man needed a helpmeet. This means there was a lack in his life and that he was not complete before bringing the woman into the picture.

A couple should complement each other they are not the same, therefore, there should be unity in diversity in trying to merge each other to one. If God wanted it so, a man would have been allowed to marry a man and vice versa but the Bible says clearly in Genesis 2:23-24 ***"And Adam said, This is now bone of my bones, and flesh of my flesh: she shall be called Woman, because she was taken out of Man . . . . Therefore shall a man leave his father and mother, and shall cleave unto his wife: and they shall be one flesh."*** This means it is a woman that must become the wife of a man. It also means they are different to each other; also they are not to change each other but to merge to each other.

Therefore having established that both are different and that both should marry each other, we can submit that when not used according to the purpose of God, the difference can cause problems.

(a) MAN'S CONSTITUTION:
A man is a being with a strong will, and an ego which wants him to be in control at all times. This ego if allowed to die, and if self-will gives way to God's will, the man's sense of direction and responsibilities can be used according to God's purpose to lead the family.

However, most men who are bereft of knowledge, whether Christian or otherwise, insist on dominating, manipulating and maltreating their wives for selfish reasons. They then go ahead to quote 1 Peter, Chapter 3:1 ***"Likewise, ye wives, be in subjection to your own husbands; that, if any obey not the word, they also may without the word be won by the conversation of the wives."*** The Bible says here that a woman must subject herself to her husband. This means, her will should be yielded like our will is yielded to the Lordship of Jesus Christ. Jesus Christ can never force himself on any person. He is too much of a gentleman. Hence women must never be repressed, subdued or harassed under the guise of submission. By your own free will, you are allowed to give your life. Nobody is forced to do so. Hence a woman, must of her own free will, submit because God commands it. The husband need not force her, she should be convinced by the fact that it is a commandment of God.

It is impossible to be one flesh with somebody who is subdued, repressed and generally oppressed; and if God says you must be one flesh, God definitely knows what he is saying. God is a God that believes in mutual submission. Jesus submitted to God to die for us on the cross of Calvary. God rewarded him by giving him a name above all names. The Holy Spirit works with the same power as the others in the Godhead. And whether you have an encounter with any of the Godhead, the result is still the same. God is an encompassing God.

This is what God expects us to do in marriage, to submit to one another. This clearly shows in the same chapter as the above 1 Peter 3:7 ***"Likewise, ye husbands, dwell with them according to*** *knowledge, giving honour unto the wife, as unto the weaker vessel, and as being heirs together of the grace of life; that your prayers be not hindered."* According to Webster's dictionary, to honour means 'Esteem accorded to virtue or talent, a public distinction or award. A public show of respect'.

When God said 'husband honour your wife', he is telling us that the erroneous ideas that a woman should be repressed, subdued, etc., is wrong. If you will show her public respect and accord her public distinction, it means that you esteem her even to be better than you. That is the way of God; and the woman too, in submitting herself esteem, the man to be better than her. This is mutual submission before God. A woman is not inferior to her husband; any such idea is a perversion of scripture. God wants a couple to be one flesh submitting to each other. Ephesians 5:21 says *"Submitting yourselves one to another in the fear of God."* For Government issues, the man is the head of the family and holds the final say under the direction of the Holy Spirit. Marriage has been referred to as a dance. The lead dancer is not necessarily the best, and the other dancers are not necessarily inferior, but it is the dance that is important not the dancers or their parts. Marriage should be seen like this.

Let us also look at an example of a larger unit like a Government. The Head of State holds the same passport as messengers, etc. It is still the passport of the nation he belongs to. He is a citizen as well as any other person; however, when there are Government issues of decision, the final ratification lies with him. In a good Government, ideas of pressure groups are collected; every citizen is allowed to contribute to the national interest and the Vice President has more contribution to give than others. Duties are shared; responsibilities are shared. The President defers to the opinion of the Vice President being more in contact with administration and people, and most of the time he just ratifies. The President of the home is the man; the woman the Vice President. The home as a Government should be such where the father, despite his air of responsibility etc., should carry his family along with compassion, love, gentleness. When he needs to be firm to ensure the corporate existence of his home, he must do so in love. This aspect of men domination and repression of women, especially in Africa, is not scriptural.

(b) **WOMAN'S CONSTITUTION:**
A woman is the weaker vessel who is very emotional; she thrives on love like a rose that is well watered. She wants to be cherished, cuddled and generally loved. She is usually sensitive. This constitution is responsible for God's instruction for God's men to love their wives and to cherish and honour them. If you honour, you cannot hurt such person easily. A woman wants her husband to be a true friend, lover, brother, father and husband. She wants somebody to look up to, to cleanse her with the word, with love, who takes control while cherishing her.

The above could complement a marriage if handled properly but it could lead to strife and contention if not properly handled. Because of a woman's constitution, the respect her husband is courting from her, could be gotten in other ways rather than the usual approach. A man can never gain the respect of his wife by ordering her to do so. Rather a man can gain the respect of his wife through the way he speaks and behaves towards her. But because the man, in his forceful way, if not submitted to God could demand respect forcefully, a woman could start to resent and even hate her husband if she sees him as being unfeeling; even though she could pretend outwardly to respect him; and they cannot be one flesh under pretence.

Some women are also very emotionally irresponsible; such women should stop being children but realise that to be one flesh is to be that, in responsibility as well as in other spheres of life. You must grow beyond the petting, the cuddling, to become a woman of virtue. A woman, as the woman referred to in Proverbs 31, whose husband's heart trusts in her. Many women cease to grow up and the childish dependent woman cannot be one flesh with her husband. It is only a woman who has achieved in spiritual matters, as well as physical, that the husband can depend on to do him good all the days of his life.

A woman's nature is normally contentious, except she has allowed renewal by the word of God. The adamic nature in a woman matters; i.e., it manifested in Eve by being argumentative and talking too much; i.e., discussion with the devil, being crafty and cunning; i.e., convincing husband to eat the forbidden fruit, being easily manipulated and also being highly emotional. The above was why it was written in Titus 2:5 **"To be discreet, chaste, keepers at home, good, obedient to their** *own husbands, that the word of God be not blasphemed."* That is why God commanded in Ephesians 5:22 *"Wives, submit yourselves unto your own husbands, as unto the Lord."* Submit to your husband, and he repeated in 1 Peter 3:1 *"Likewise, ye wives, be in subjection to your own husbands; that, if any obey not the word, they also may without the word be won by the conversation of the wives."* That wives should be subject to their husbands in all things, because God knows their constitution, and to protect them he put somebody above them with power of decision, to sober down the high emotions of a woman.

As far as God is concerned, man is the head of the woman, and a woman is commanded to obey God by being subject to his authority. However, because of education, many women refuse to do this. This indicates that they are not obeying God and as it is said in Leviticus, such a woman is under a curse because she is walking contrary to God. Leviticus 26:27-28 says *"And if ye will not for all this hearken unto me, but walk contrary unto me; . . . Then I will walk contrary unto you also in fury; and I, even I, will chastise you seven times for your sins."*

Women should take note because it is possible for a woman to be successful in spiritual matters and still be a failure in her marriage. The person is a spirit, soul and body. The spirit could be a success and the soul and body a failure, if the spirit is not allowed to renew the soul and body with the word of God. Moses did not enter the promised land, but he made heaven. His spirit was successful but his soul was a failure; anger prevented him from being successful in entering the promised land.

Many times a man/woman constitution prevents them from making a success of their secular life, but they would still be Christians. In Isaiah 3:6,7,12, the Bible says ***"When a man shall take hold of his brother, of the house of his father, saying, Thou hast clothing, be thou our ruler, and let this ruin be under thy hand: . . . In that day shall he swear, saying, I will not be an healer; for in my house is neither bread nor clothing: make me not a ruler of the people . . . As for my people, children are their oppressors, and women rule over them. O my people, they which lead thee cause thee to err, and destroy the way of thy paths."*** God made it clear that women are not expected to rule over men in the home.

Hence women should realise that God understands their constitution and he knows what he has deposited in men before he made them the leaders. With apologies to women's liberation, I believe as women, we should not be abused, disrespected, but honoured as weaker vessels as the Bible says. We have manifold duties, we are the spinal cord of the body that carries signals to all parts of the body. The spinal cord should not fight to be the head, because in many instances it is more useful; but both cannot do without each other. That is what is meant by being one body, one flesh. Mature inter-dependence and acknowledgement of individual roles, as God has ordained it. One is not inferior to another, but one is to head; one carries the responsibility of leadership while the other is supportive but almost more important in the area of responsibility.

God protects us from our weaknesses; he created us and he knows how we can operate effectively. Left to man, he could live life without intimacy or love, hence God commanded him to love his wife. Left to woman, she feels that her intuition and emotion can direct her effectively. That was why God commanded her to submit to her husband. Hence the two parts are not inferior to one another. Let the word dwell richly in you and renew your soul. Your soul is made up of your intellect, will and mind, and this is filled up by the type of education you had, your upbringing and hereditary factors.

All these three things need to be cleaned out and renewed by the word of God; become a new creation and you will see that you are made in a form after Christ, and it is possible to walk as children of light, living in mutual love and submission after the likeness of God.

CHILDREN:

Children could prevent a couple from being one flesh. The couple must always have in perspective that they are one, and the children are the extension of that one. Some men develop relationships with their first male child; seeing them as an extension of themselves; and once these children start growing up, they neglect their wife. This happened to Isaac in the case of Esau.

Esau was the first son, and according to their tradition the first son has the right of leadership. Secondly he was a good hunter and Isaac ate his venison; hence he loved him. This divided their family. Rebbeca loved Jacob and the family was divided into two.

In Christian marriage, children must see their parents as one and the children as an extension. No partiality, favouritism is allowed in a marriage after God's heart. Many women also abandon their husband and make them loveless, once the children start to come. This is not according to the word of God. The husband must be first, and the children come after.

The discipline of the children must be done as one flesh. The Bible instructs fathers in Ephesians 6:4 by saying ***"And, ye fathers, provoke not your children to wrath: but bring them up in the nurture and admonition of the Lord."*** And mothers in Proverbs 29:15 by saying ***"The rod and reproof give wisdom; but a child left to himself bringeth his mother to shame."*** It is important for both parents to discipline their children. If one parent refuses and becomes a friend to the child, as some mothers do, when the father is disciplining the child, they will end up spoiling the children's life. So children must see their parents as one flesh, and parents must refuse to allow any kind of separation because of children, rather the love and unity should be stronger, so that as a body they bring up the children in the fear of God.

EXTERNAL FACTORS:

Most of the external factors affecting marriage have been listed in chapter two. These, we discussed as areas to be unified before a husband and wife can become one flesh; they are, friends, family, work, church activities, hobbies, etc. All these areas, if not united as discussed in chapter two, can put the marriage asunder. To disallow the above factors from putting the marriage asunder, adjustment, communication and implementation must take place.

Another set of external factors can be identified as spiritual forces; these manifest through demonic activities, which can be associated to the supernatural. This can be introduced by association with witches and wizards; those who employ the use of sorcerers, enchanters, etc. These associations can be either with family members or colleagues or neighbours. The only solution to this kind of external attack is found in 2 Corinthians 10:4 *"(For the weapons of our warfare are not carnal, but mighty through God to the pulling down of strong holds;)"*. Prayer is the solution and this should be done by speaking the word of God to pull down the strongholds of the enemy. By using all the weapons listed above to overcome.

Another external factor that can put a family asunder and prevent the oneness of a couple, is sexual immorality, either in thought, word or deed. We will look closely at this in the next chapter.

Chapter Four

ONE FLESH

To be one flesh in marriage, is to walk in the counsel of God. It is to attain the standards that God has ordained for marriage. A standard where self-consciousness and selfishness gives way to God-consciousness and unity under the control of God.

At this point, the couple seeks to satisfy any commandment of God and forget their individual self to make sure they attain this and every other commandment of God. Very few people get there. (The Bible says in Hebrews 13:4 ***"Marriage is honourable in all, and the bed undefiled: but whoremongers and adulterer God will judge."*** That marriage is honourable in all, tells us that marriage in all areas is supposed to be an honourable estate; but unfortunately, all have sinned and fallen short of the glory of God. What God wants to be honourable, to use as an example of making man a model of his character in love, unity, harmony, kindness, may be used to dishonour God and disappoint him if one is not careful.

If you abuse the institution of marriage, which God says is honourable, you are walking contrary to God, and God can never be pleased with you until you restitute. God expects high standards from his own people in marriage, as well as in sexual relationships. This is why the Bible says the bed is undefiled. No way for adultery.

One flesh is two becoming one. In God's agenda, there is no room for sexual immorality, because this topic of immorality is a major stumbling block to becoming one flesh. We will look closely at sexual purity.

SEXUAL PURITY:
In Hebrew 13:4, the Bible says *"Marriage is honourable in all, and the bed undefiled: but whoremongers and adulterers God will judge."*
God says he will judge whoremongers and adulterers. God expects believers to be pure, both morally and sexually. In Matthew 5:8, the Bible says *"Blessed are the pure in heart: for they shall see God."* Jesus told us clearly that only the pure in heart shall see God; hence it is immaterial whether you actually commit adultery or fornication at all, so far, your heart is impure. You have fallen short of God's standard; you cannot see God. Furthermore, with an impure heart, you can never reach the standard of God in marriage, of being one flesh with your spouse, because it is in attaining the perfection that is in Christ Jesus, that one can become one flesh with another human being. Being dead to self and alive in the spirit. The word pure or chaste means to be free from all taint of lewdness; it means one will totally avoid all acts, thoughts and words that could incite any desire which is not in line with one's marital vows.

A couple are expected to have self-control and restraint from everything that can taint, excite, defile, inspire desire or cheapen their purity before God. The devil is always fighting through perverted inclination and earthly enjoyment to subject a man to the lowest level of spiritual existence. He knows that this cheapens man and his purity before God, because God is pure; hence any man that God will give the gift of being one flesh with his wife, must be sexually pure. He must be able to control his body in sanctification and honour. 1 Thessalonians 4:4, *"That every one of you should know how to possess his vessel in sanctification and honour."*

The Bible is clear on adultery. In Exodus 20:14, *"Thou shalt not commit adultery."* God gave a clear commandment against it. This is the seventh commandment and it encompasses immorality and all sexual sins. Adultery means unfaithfulness to one's spouse. It was punishable by death in the Old Testament, and it amounts to despising God as David was told in the Bible, 2 Samuel 12:9-10. *"Wherefore hast thou despised the commandment of the Lord, to do evil in his sight? Thou hast killed Uriah the Hittite with the sword, and hast taken his wife to be thy wife, and hast slain him with the sword of the children of Ammon . . . Now therefore the sword shall never depart from thine house; because thou hast despised me, and hast taken the wife of Uriah the Hittite to be thy wife."* Adultery begins by a desire in the heart. So before a man commits adultery, he must already have committed adultery against God in his heart, (by not being faithful to

God); thereby despising God and his commandments.

Job realised this when he said in Job 31:1,7,8,9a, *"I made a covenant with mine eyes; why then should I think upon a maid? . . . If my step hath turned out of the way, and mine heart walked after mine eyes, and if any blot hath cleaved to mine hands; . . . Then let me sow, and let another eat; yea let my offspring be rooted out. . . . If mine heart have been deceived by a woman."* Here Job was talking of his integrity and his adherence and faithfulness to God and his ways. He spoke of his innocence in the sins of the heart, which includes sexual lust, impure thought and looking at women to lust.

The Bible tells us in Hebrews 12:14, *"Follow peace with all men, and holiness, without which no man shall see the Lord."* And in 1 Corinthians 6:19 the Bible says *"What! know ye not that your body is the temple of the Holy Ghost, which is in you, which ye have of God, and ye are not your own?"* We are being told that holiness is the most important thing in our walk with God, and obedience to his commandments. God cannot behold iniquity.

A couple must be holy before they can be one flesh; they must have put flesh and all its impure works to death, and constantly walk in the spirit. They must be pure before God.

CONCLUSION

Genesis 2:23-24 says *"**And Adam said, This is now bone of my bones, and flesh of my flesh: she shall be called Woman, because she was taken out of Man . . . Therefore shall a man leave his father and his mother, and shall cleave unto his wife: and they shall be one flesh.**"*

(1) What Adam said in verse 23 means he had a revelation. Before you can walk in the purpose of God for marriage, every man/woman must get a revelation of the fact that his wife/husband is now bone of his bones and flesh of his flesh. It is because many men/women have not got the revelation that there are problems in their homes. You must come to the reality of the fact that God has given you a wife/husband meant for you and she/he is not going anywhere; she/he is part of you, her/his happiness means your happiness; then you will now settle down.

(2) In verse 24, it says a man shall leave; at this time there was no father or mother but for posterity God made it clear that a man must leave. If a man doesn't leave he cannot be one

flesh. He must leave all the most important of which is the father and mother.
(3) He must cleave to his wife, by moulding his life achievement, friends, etc., to be interwoven with her own so that they can holdfast and stick together.
(4) And they shall be one flesh after the first three steps. God will then grant the gift of being one flesh with one another. It is a spiritual union, a merging together that only our God can do. When this happens, the family become a praise on earth and a family after God's own heart, likeness and character.

For counselling write:

Mrs T. O. Oluwadare,
No. 372 Water Gardens,
Burwood Place,
London, W2 2DJ.